The Screenwriting Quick Start

Basics of Development, Politics,
Networking, and More
in a One-Night Read

Rich Whiteside

The Screenwriting Quick Start

All rights reserved
Copyright © 2017 by Rich Whiteside

ISBN: 978-0-9992745-0-7

No part of this publication may be reproduced, stored in a retrieval system, or transmitted in any form or by any means electronic, mechanical, photocopying, recording, or otherwise, without the written permission of the author or publisher.

Contents

Introduction v

Chapter One: Skill Sets 1

Chapter Two: Approaches to Story Structuring 13

Chapter Three: Training for Screenwriters 21

Chapter Four: Developing Your Screenwriting Style 27

Chapter Five: Production Development 31

Chapter Six: Basic Hollywood Politics 47

Chapter Seven: Networking 57

Chapter Eight: Goal Setting and Successful Writing
                   Habits for Screenwriters 63

Chapter Nine: Support Communities 69

Chapter Ten: Commonly Debated Topics 71

Conclusion 79

Introduction

In these pages are insights I wish had been available to me when I began my screenwriting journey—they would have saved me from a number of missteps. A vital part of career building in any industry is effectively playing the political game. However, to play the game effectively, you must first understand the game. In this book, I've condensed down what I have learned through twenty-eight years of incredible and career-dashing experiences working in and around Hollywood to provide a basic understanding of what I now know about how the industry works.

This book is for those who lack industry contacts. Those who are connected have far more viable options for learning and launching a career than those of us who have none.

This book is intentionally short to follow my number one technical-writing rule: be clear, concise, and compelling. It's also short because you don't need to be an expert storyteller to begin your screenwriting life, nor an expert in industry politics to launch a career. To be a screenwriter, write and don't stop. To launch a career, a basic understanding of where the potholes lay and landmines are buried is indispensable.

My focus is on helping you decide where to best invest your time, money, and effort and where not to waste your time, money, and effort. You'll gain insights on screenwriting skill sets, story structuring approaches, development, politics, networking, goal setting, and more. While I do embellish a bit here and there, I've edited to keep the rhetoric minimal.

The overarching reality of Hollywood careers is that exceedingly few work full time. Most who work in the industry have full-time jobs outside Hollywood that allow them to take on the occasional industry jobs, when they come. It makes no difference whether you are a writer, actor, director, cinematographer, or any other artisan. The preponderance of industry people land work only intermittently and therefore need a highly flexible outside income stream (basically, a day job) to pursue their dream. Thus, all the jokes about being a writer/waiter. Accept this reality and plan accordingly.

One unfortunate truth about launching and maintaining a career is that, too often, success depends on factors outside of your control—it's often about politics and timing. In one instance, timing led to one of my screenplays being optioned. A director was quickly attached, and it moved toward production. A couple of months later, politics killed the project when an unexpected threat of a Screen Actors Guild strike (from the commercial division) hit the news. That loss cost me a half-a-million-dollar payday plus WGA rewriting fees. Timing and politics are out of your control. All you can do is put yourself in the best position to win. So, part of my message is to not waste time dwelling on aspects of career-building that are out of your control. Instead, put your efforts into activities that will give you the best chance to realize your dream.

When it comes to writing, the most important edict I can pass on is to write. Write every day. A daily writing habit is the gym workout that is essential to grow as a writer and compete. An athlete cannot be competitive unless he or she commits to a regular training routine. Imagine an athlete who trains only every now and then and expects to win at the highest levels. It's not going to happen. Also, don't fall into the trap of feeling that you are growing as a writer if all you do is study how-to books and attend screenwriting conferences. Unless you are writing, you are not growing. Writing is the true teacher. Focus on writing first.

The first action most aspiring screenwriters take is to buy a how-to book, and each year selecting that book becomes harder as more new books flood the marketplace. The chapter on structure will help you identify which broad approach to structuring is likely to work best for you. Given that insight, you will be better able to filter through the pile of books to select one that best resonates with you. While I do mention books that have greatly influenced me, I do not recommend any particular one on how to structure a story because, from my point of view, that first book is best if it matches how much hand-holding you need. Some writers only want to know the basics and then be left alone to get at it. Others want a complete step-by-step roadmap. Others need something in between. The chapter on structure will help you determine which lane in the road is best for you. Whatever approach you choose, it should be one that will get you writing, keep you writing, and pull the creative best out of you. This is the best value of a how-to book.

Some Hollywood writers claim never to have read a screenwriting book or taken a screenwriting class. These are people who find that books and classroom learning fail to motivate them or inspire their creativity—they are at their creative best by working from the gut. They learned this craft by writing and getting feedback from experienced writers. In the end, they learned the same storytelling principles taught in the books and schools, but they succeeded because they do the one thing that the preponderance of aspiring writers fail to do: they write and kept writing. Others need a proven path to follow, and without a path they remain dormant. What gets you writing?

No matter which approach works best for you, writers write. As Lew Hunter advises in his book *Lew Hunter's Screenwriting 434*, "Learn to swim in the deepest part of the pool."

In the long run, I believe the more approaches to story development and writing styles you become familiar with, the more unique and polished your storytelling will become. Your writing style (your writing voice, as some refer to it) will come out of a balance of writing, reading produced and unproduced scripts, and studying books on screenwriting.

I love the study of writing and, admittedly, I have invested an excessive amount of time studying the many approaches to storytelling and story structuring. My dedication to this is not remotely necessary to turning out quality scripts, but I am fascinated with how writers create, and you can benefit from my obsession.

So, who am I to have written this book? I come to this with multiple levels of industry experience: writer, actor, journalist, subject matter expert and more than a decade of work at a major studio in Network Television Business Affairs and Legal. That being said, first and foremost, I am a writer, screenwriter and an avid screenwriting student. As a professional writer, I've been a technical and journalistic writer for more than thirty years. I have written or co-written a couple of dozen screenplays and have contributed story elements and subject-matter expertise to prime-time television shows. As a screenwriting journalist, I have interviewed more than a hundred writers, producers, directors, studio executives, agents, screenwriting professors, and authors of popular screenwriting how-to books. I have written for *Script* magazine (when it was in print), screenwriting newsletters and screenwriting websites, and authored the book *The Screenwriting Life*.

Over the past twenty-eight years, I have had a fascination with story structuring. I've studied all the major schools of thought about structure, first to absorb the philosophy and second to determine how that philosophy can enhance my writing process and style. My office bookshelves are filled with screenwriting how-to books—heavily underlined—including many lesser known books, some dating back to the start of filmmaking. As to formal training, I completed three years in the UCLA Advanced Professional Program in Screenwriting and briefly studied the USC World Building approach. It is from this broad experience that I have written *The Screenwriting Quick Start*.

One final piece of advice. A close acting friend, former Army Ranger, Tim Abell, advised a group of aspiring actors—who were bitterly complaining about not landing television and film roles—that if they wanted to act, they should get out and act and stop whining about not landing Screen Actors Guild (SAG) jobs. They should act anywhere and everywhere they could, whether they were paid or not. They should act because it was in their DNA to do it, and to let the journey of learning, performing, and growing as an actor lead the way to potentially being cast in film and television. He warned that if they were only pursuing acting to land big-payday gigs, they were on the path to failure and should go home then and there. This advice applies to screenwriters as well. Write. Establish a daily habit. Write because you have stories in you that must come out. Don't write to chase a payday, because that intent will show in your writing and stifle your career aspirations.

One final warning as you read, you will find repetition of points between chapters and within chapters because I wrote each chapter and some sections within chapters to act as a standalone on specific subjects. I felt this was important because that not every reader will want or need to read every chapter.

Now, read on. But more importantly, as my mentor Lew Hunter always signs off:

Write on!

Chapter One

SKILL SETS

On your screenwriting journey, you'll need to master at least six fundamental screenwriting skill sets:

- Story structuring

- Character development

- Dialogue

- Exposition

- Action-description writing

- Screenplay formatting

In your lifetime, you have seen, read or heard thousands upon thousands of stories. This means you come to screenwriting and storytelling with an innate sense of what works as a marketable story, and you surely have an opinion about what you like and don't like. Trust your instincts. However, what is a marketable mainstream script and what you like might not match up. If this is the case, prepare for a greater struggle than most. Regardless, instinct will be one of your most valuable assets.

Having a sense of what you like in a story is great, but it's rarely enough to carry you through to writing a marketable screenplay right out of the gate. You will probably need to study storytelling and screenwriting techniques. As you start your screenwriting life, write, read scripts (produced and unproduced), study screenwriting how-to books, take classes, attend seminars, and join writers' groups. Fully engage in the community as much as you can.

When it comes to skill sets, the good news is that, as you start out, you will probably discover you have a natural talent in one or two of these skill sets. However, I have yet to meet a first-time screenwriter who was gifted in all of them. So, accept that you will have to become a student of screenwriting and storytelling, become a student of the business, and develop some skill sets.

A script is a blueprint for making a movie. It is essentially a technical document used by production company departments to determine all the elements needed to make the movie. This is called breaking down a script. Knowing the department involved in the breakdown process will give you an idea of some of the information a script must convey: Location scouts determine what locations they must find. The casting department determines what roles to cast, which requires knowing the age and other character specifications. The prop master determines what props are needed. The special effects masters determine the effects needed. The set dressers determine what they will need to dress each location (all the minutiae in a setting that the actors don't use as props but that add ambiance to the location). And actors study their characters' dialogue and glean character and other background information from the script to better understand their characters' motivations.

A screenplay must accomplish all this while telling a compelling story, and do it within a limited number of pages. Properly formatted, a tightly written speculation movie script (a.k.a. a spec script—a script written in hopes of selling it) should run 105–110 pages for a drama and about 95 pages for a comedy. However, page count is one of the hotly debated subjects in the world of amateur scriptwriting. Some camps allow up to 120 pages. I recommend you shoot for 105–110. Each script page should represent about a minute of screen time. However, in television, this rule does not hold. In fact, there is little correlation between a television script page count and screen time. I regularly see television drama scripts of 60 pages or more that translate to about forty-five minutes of on-screen story. But for feature films, the rule holds.

With that in mind, let's move forward into the skill sets of scriptwriting.

STORY STRUCTURE

Structure refers to the framework of a story—how a story unfolds—and structuring refers to the process of taking an initial, compelling idea and developing a complete story from that idea. That is, coming up with the scenes that connect one to the next to create the journey. The three basic components of story structure are plot (the actions and events of the story as they play out from beginning to end), subplots (small stories within the larger story) and character development (characters' emotional growth, if any, and relationships with other characters). The genre you are writing (action, drama, comedy, crime, fantasy, etc.) will have unique structuring elements that you must address. Screenwriting guru John Truby offers a wealth of training on specific genres. Admittedly, structuring is far more than these three elements, but this is enough of a foundational understanding for the purposes of this book.

One motivation for writing this Quick Start is to provide clarity for those just starting down the screenwriting path regarding the competing schools of thought about structure. There is an abundance of screenwriting how-to books out there, many with wildly differing approaches to developing a story. Picking an approach to start your screenwriting life with tends to be the first major frustration for new screenwriters. Ultimately, I believe it's worthwhile to learn from many points of view and to broaden your knowledge. In a later chapter, the basic approaches to story structuring are addressed.

CHARACTER DEVELOPMENT

Character development is one of the most complex and challenging aspects of storytelling. Populate your stories with exciting, compelling characters, and a story takes on far greater appeal. So then, what is character? What makes one character more engaging than another?

"Character" is more than dialogue and quirky mannerisms; it also includes how a character thinks, walks, talks, dresses, and physically interacts with others. To get a solid foundational understanding of character development, I recommend Lajos Egri's book *The Art of Dramatic Writing*. He has a highly detailed section on character development. He also has wonderful thoughts on premise (what the story is about; your message) and character arcs (how a character changes emotionally from the beginning of the story to the end). I often warn people that if they read his book, they might find themselves scared to write, because they will become aware of how much effort they can and should put into story development.

Too often, beginning writers think of crafting characters only in terms of naming the protagonist (the Hero) and the antagonist (the Villain or opposing force) and giving each some unique, if not quirky, physicality and dialogue; they pretty much stop there. While these are important elements, to write compelling stories, it requires a far more nuanced expression of character. It's likely that the stories you love are your favorites in large part because of the compelling character relationships and not the convoluted plots. My favorite screenwriting edict is: Write simple stories (plots) with complex characters. If you go down the path of attempting to craft a complex plot with complex characters, you'll discover you won't have enough pages to fully develop both and stay within the standard script length. I highly recommend that when you start writing your first scripts that you adhere to the adage of: Simple stories with complex characters.

One exception to this edict is the genre of action films. In the action genre, the compelling element that consumes page count is, of course, the action. That's why, in my opinion, action stories require simple action plots with simple characters to have the page space to write the action elements.

Egri teaches that each character must have a physiological, sociological and psychological element. To write a character well, you must know why he or she makes the choices he or she does. Those choices must be believable to your audience. Otherwise, the choices tend to feel random and inconsistent, and that can make an audience feel manipulated rather than entertained.

DIALOGUE

The challenge of writing movie dialogue is that it must sound like ordinary dialogue but do so much more. Dialogue should move the plot along, provide character illumination, entertain, and so on. Many first-time writers fill pages with superfluous banter that mimics real life but doesn't serve any of the above that dialogue should fulfill. The dialogue just fills pages.

One of the first rules you learn about writing a scene is to start the scene as late in the action as possible and get out of the scene at the first possible chance. This applies to movie dialogue as well. For example, notice that in movies today, characters get to the point quickly. They rarely say "hello" or "goodbye"—they tend to get right into the situation—or their greetings are clipped; they are snippets of social norms. This is because screen time is valuable, and screen time spent saying, "Hi, how are you?" is better spent advancing the story.

A critical element of dialogue is subtext. An excellent book on the subject is *Writing Subtext: What lies beneath* by Dr. Linda Seger. She explains that, "Subtext is the true meaning simmering underneath the words and actions." The deepest emotional conflicts in a story often play out in subtext. Maybe the greatest challenge for people in real life (and with fictional characters) is using and understanding subtext. Here are a couple of questions to consider as you craft dialogue with subtext: How effectively does your character use subtext to achieve his or her goals? How effective is your character at understanding and dealing with subtext? What does that say about your character's character?

Subtext involves the audience in the story by forcing viewers to work a bit to read between the lines—to figure out what is really going on. If your characters say exactly what they mean, your audience is not being challenged to use their brain. With judicious use of subtext, movie audiences become more engaged in a story and that raises the level of their enjoyment.

While we're talking about subtext, subtext is not limited to dialogue, a character's actions or inactions can convey subtext as well. By the way, actors look for subtext to layer into their performance. If you don't provide it, the well-trained actor will make subtext acting choices to give their performance depth and nuance. You will want actors to contribute artistically to the collaborative process, but don't give them a dry desert of subtextless dialogue and actions to work from.

EXPOSITION

Exposition is background information that an audience needs to engage with the characters, their struggles and to care about the outcome of the story. This includes information about the world of the story, past events, the characters' backgrounds and their relationships (including the history of those relationships). Exposition can be visual: for example, the beginning scrolls in the *Star Wars* movies, the use of photographs, trophies, or even a certificate seen on a wall. Exposition can be pure information delivered through dialogue. When Hollywood people talk about exposition, they are generally referring to expositional dialogue. Try to avoid pure dialogue-driven exposition scenes as much as possible because it is the most boring of methods to deliver backstory information.

Your experiences in life have shaped your life choices and the relationships you have, for good or ill. When you meet up with someone you know, your history with that person shapes the way you act and converse. The relationship is already emotionally charged to some degree. Someone who doesn't know you, when observing the interaction, might not get the subtleties of the conversation. However, if the observer understood the history of your relationship, he or she might be more engaged in the interaction. Exposition provides the audience with that kind of background information so that actions and interactions take on greater meaning.

One guideline for expositional dialogue is that it is best expressed through conflict, or as some prefer to express it, through tension in the scene. It is conflict that engages and holds an audience's attention. Instead of having characters matter-of-factly pass information to each other and, thereby, to the audience, add tension to the scene as they do that.

Through expositional dialogue, you can make a statement about a character's attitudes. Well-placed exposition can add a kick to the story's impact. Poorly choreographed exposition muddies the script's read and the movie's viewing. Exposition that comes out too early or too late in a story can confuse or frustrate your audience. A good rule of thumb is to introduce exposition at the point in the story it is needed by the characters and the audience—not before. Screenwriters writing their first scripts too often jam all the exposition up front in the action-description instead of pacing it out as needed.

As you watch movies and television shows, note how the writer(s) conveys exposition to you, how that placement engages you further in the story, pulls you out of the story, or confuses you. Note how the writer(s) build tension into exposition scenes.

In an action story, you often get a pure exposition scene at the beginning of the story in which one character briefs another character (or a team) about a situation. Usually, these scenes are boring, even with tension, but sometimes it is the most expedient way to get enough initial backstory out to quickly launch the journey. This type of straightforward background information scene is commonplace in procedural television shows as well as action movies. J.J. Abrams' writing staff on *Alias* often married an exposition scene with an action scene. A briefing would start and then the visuals would move to an action sequence relating to the information being briefed with the briefing continuing as a voice over through the beginning of the action scene. A wonderful way to make exposition interesting and immediately connected to the story.

Exposition might be a scene in a love story where we learn something important about one or both lovers that helps us understand why they act the way they do or why they are a perfect fit for each other. There is an art to the exposition scene. An example of an expositional scene I like is the opening sequence in *Unforgiven* when the William Munny character is introduced. In this short scene, you learn all you need to know at that point in the story about William Munny and the journey he is about to take. Later in the story, more exposition is revealed about him as well as historical insights about Western gunslingers. For me, this movie stands out in the deft way the writer used exposition to add depth and nuance in a tension-filled scene.

One form of expositional dialogue is banter—the pithy, back-and-forth quips between characters. Banter might appear to be frivolous bits of comic relief, but at its core, it is exposition. For example, two characters with contrasting life experiences, philosophies about life, and personalities rib each other about their differences in a pseudo-aggressive buddy-buddy manner. Through this exchange, the writer informs the audience about the characters, their backgrounds, and potentially about story and relationship situations that are in play.

Now that you are aware of exposition, look for it in everything you watch or read.

ACTION-DESCRIPTION

Action-description is the prose-writing element of a screenplay—the novel-like element of the script. At its best, this style of writing is terse—it's novel-like writing without the flourish. When you read a script, this is the prose outside the lines of dialogue. If you've read a script, this will be clear. If you haven't read a script, you can easily find PDFs of scripts online.

One guideline about action-description writing is that it should be limited to describing what can be seen or heard. Because movies are manipulation of light and sound, the action-description should primarily be limited to describing actions, visuals and non-verbal sounds. Avoid writing in the action-description how characters feel, what they think, or historical information that is not provided directly to a viewing audience. Routinely, first-time scriptwriters tell the reader in action-description about past events that shape the current situation without conveying that information to a movie audience through dialogue or action. Unless there is a way to portray that information on screen, there is no way for a viewing audience to know this information, and it is wasted description that only benefits a reader. Great for novels. Bad for scripts.

The guideline in screenwriting is if you need to convey what a character is feeling or thinking, before you do that through dialogue, it is best to express it through an action, visual, or non-verbal sound (in the action-description). However, there will be places where it will be useful for clarity to indicate a character's emotion, especially, as it applies to dialogue. When this is necessary, the emotion is added in a parenthetical before a speech. This is often referred to as a "wryly" because beginning screenwriters seem to feel compelled to constantly direct the actor by indicating the emotion the actor is to use when delivering the lines, and the most common parenthetical is wryly. Thus, the reference. Don't use this option as a crutch to get around writing quality, emotion-filled dialogue. Also, too many "wrylies" will eat up page space that is better used to develop the story. Above all else, keep your action-description tight, without the flowery adjectives and adverbs you use in a novel.

The challenge for most beginning screenwriters is to keep the action-description minimal and engaging, in a way that moves the story forward. The reason for the terseness, as you might guess, is that the page count of a modern spec script is limited to 105–110 pages. Whether you are writing for television or a feature-film, you do not have the page space to wax poetic as you would in a novel. Make your point. Make it quickly. Make it intriguing. Keep the story turning until you reach The End.

The great screenwriters have an art and elegance to their action-description writing. Read scripts written by top screenwriters and you'll discover this for yourself. Having said the above about terse writing, don't worry about that in your first draft. Use your editing process to tighten the action-description. Just be aware that in the end, action-description writing should be terse.

RECOMMENDATION: As I've said repeatedly, read produced scripts and note the choices the writer (or writing team) has made in action-description writing. One exercise I used to hone my screenwriting skill sets was to retype precisely the first five pages of screenplays written by the most successful writers of the day. This drill helped me develop my own writing style. I noted the style they used to keep the word count down while keeping me thoroughly engaged. This drill might not be for you, but I'm a detail-oriented person, and it was an invaluable experience.

SCREENPLAY FORMATTING

Script formatting rules help make it easier for production departments to determine their responsibilities. The basic screenplay elements are slug lines (scene headings that tell whether the scene is inside or outside, the specific location and whether it is night or day), action-description writing, character names, dialogue and transitions between scenes. Other information that might be noted in scripts are props (weapons, musical instruments, tools, etc.) and, for some, unique sounds. Don't worry about the rules; there are books that give you the guidelines, and screenwriting software programs provide examples and automatically format the key elements as you write. Just be aware that there are basic formatting style guidelines for writing scripts.

Remember, a script serves to tell a compelling story and acts as a blueprint for producing the movie. That's your challenge.

Chapter Two

APPROACHES TO STORY STRUCTURING

Structure refers to the framework of a story—how a story unfolds—and structuring refers to the process of taking an initial, compelling idea and developing a complete story from that idea.

Having studied many dozens of story structuring approaches (through books, in-class training, seminars and conferences), I have concluded that all styles of structure fall into one of three over-arching approaches: The Three-Act Structure, Scene Sequencing, or what I call the Roadmap. Each approach has the capacity to deliver a marketable story. Become familiar with all three approaches, but for now, focus on one that best suits your needs. The primary selection question is: How much hand-holding do you want—the least possible (three act structure), a moderate amount (scene sequencing), or a most (the roadmap)?

This chapter provides you with some context so you can choose the structuring style that best suits your writing style and work habits right now. As you grow as a writer, your needs are likely to change, but right now you're not picking an approach that will serve you best when you are more experienced. You're picking an approach that will get you writing and keep you writing now.

Warning: If you ask members of screenwriting groups for a book recommendation, you'll get an earful of conflicting opinions. In fact, nowhere will you find more heated arguments than when you raise the subject of story structuring in any writers' group and ask for a book recommendation. It seems that no two screenwriters can agree on which book is the best. The only other arena that provokes such emotion is martial arts. Ask any martial arts student about his or her style, and you will be told in no uncertain terms that their style is "the one, and the only one" and that all the other styles should be banned from existence and their practitioners sent directly to hell. This is how strongly many screenwriters feel about their chosen structuring approach (usually, a specific book they hold sacred).

When it comes to telling a story, accept that you already have a strong opinion about what you like and don't like. However, it takes more than good instincts for a beginning screenwriter to flesh out an idea into a complete, fully-expressed story. Without a structuring process, most first-time screenwriters run out of steam well before The End, or their finished scripts turn out bland. In response to the millions of aspiring writers seeking help, and, invariably, too often, seeking a quick how-to-write-a-story template, a never-ending stream of books, seminars, and conferences on the theme of structure have hit the marketplace. This is not a put down of books or seminars, I have indulged in all of these and thoroughly loved the experience and come away the richer for the experience. For those coming to screenwriting, it's become a bit overwhelming to determine where to start; where to invest their time and money. When I started, there was one book in bookstores, Syd Field's *Screenplay*.

Why is structuring a story necessary? Why can't you just come up with an idea and wing it? Well, some can. Most can't. My experience has been that untrained writers who winging it invariably end up completely dead-ended halfway through a complete script. What commonly happens is that the first scene—based on a highly charged idea—is exciting, passion-filled, and a breeze to write. The next scene is still strongly motivated and relatively easy to write, but not quite as effortless as the first. The scene after that is a little harder to write and less inspired. Then each successive scene diminishes in passion and ease of writing until the plot grinds to a halt, generally about midway in the page count. In a feature-length screenplay, that is about page sixty. The value of a structuring approach is it provides a process to flesh out a fully-developed story and to come up with the scenes necessary to fill all the pages necessary.

Learning the process of structuring is best done through a combination of writing, study and reading produced scripts. Again, writing is vital to mastering. Don't be seduced into the trap of either believing that it is better to read and memorize multiple how-to books on screenwriting structuring before you write, or ignoring all advice and trying to figure it out on your own. For whatever reason, some writers don't want to be "tainted" by teaching—they want to be "totally original." In my opinion, this is like setting out to become a great painter but refusing to learn from or study the masters.

Below is an overview of the three approaches to structure described earlier. Once you have figured out which approach best inspires you, engage with a teacher, school, or book that teaches that approach, and write!

THE THREE-ACT APPROACH
(ARISTOTELIAN "BEGINNING-MIDDLE-END")

The three-act structure is based on Aristotle's *Poetics* and is the least constrained approach. Aristotle teaches that a story has a distinct beginning, middle, and end. This is commonly referred to as a "three-act structure." However, the "three-act" label sometimes confuses people when they read or hear of plays or television shows that have two, four, five, six, or more "acts." This is an apples-and-oranges comparison. Three-act structure simply means that you can break your storytelling into a story beginning, a story middle, and a story end. A television show might have four, five, or six acts, but these act breaks are for commercials—it's about profit. Most plays are written and performed in two acts with an intermission between. Regardless of how you break up a story for pauses—commercial breaks for television or an intermissions for a play—every story can be viewed as having a clear beginning, middle, and end.

The beginning (the situation) informs the audience about the world of the story, the rules of that world (e.g., if there is magic, establish that; if it's a military setting or an organized crime world, establish that), the physical setting, the key characters (specifically, the protagonist and the antagonist) and the major relationships and conflicts; the beginning also sets up the themes of the story and establishes the central problem. That's a lot to accomplish to set up your story.

The middle (the complications) is where the protagonist and antagonist maneuver to defeat the other. This is also where the story themes are richly explored and where the strengths and determination (physical, mental, moral) of the protagonist and antagonist are pitted against each other.

Typically, the protagonist tries a simple solution to resolve the problem but it fails miserably and creates more complications for the protagonist. In general, in the middle, things get in the way. To make the story interesting, the antagonist should be, at the least, equally matched with the protagonist. To be compelling, the antagonist should be the more powerful, the more ruthless, of the two, but of lesser moral fiber.

The end (the conclusion) is where the central problem is resolved in a compelling way. In a love story, the lovers come together. In an action story, the protagonist wins, the crisis is resolved, and the world comes into a new balance . . . until the next crisis.

As to the ratio of pages in these three acts: broadly speaking, the beginning is one-quarter or less of the length of the whole story, the middle is the bulk of it, at least half of the overall length, and the end is quick, one-quarter or less. Some experts teach a quick ending sequence of about an eighth of the total page count.

The most prominent screenwriting book that teaches the Aristotelian point of view is Lew Hunter's *Screenwriting 434*. Professor Hunter was the co-chair of the UCLA Masters in Screenwriting program. In his book, he walks the reader through the ten-week UCLA Screenwriting 434 class, in which students move from story idea to a first-draft script in ten weeks. He firmly believes that marketable, modern stories are balanced on two pillars: Aristotle's beginning, middle, and end, and Lajos Egri's sense of character, as presented in his book *The Art of Dramatic Writing*. Master's students take the 434 class multiple times. Hunter also teaches that it might take writing as many as ten or more screenplays to properly grasp all the skill sets of a working screenwriter well enough to be turning out solid scripts.

THE SCENE SEQUENCING APPROACH

Scene Sequencers view a complete story as a series of scene-sequence short stories that link and build to tell the complete story. The number of scenes in a sequence is not a fixed number—it depends upon how many scenes the writer needs to accomplish the sequence. As far as the total number of scenes in a standard movie script, a drama feature script generally has about thirty major scenes and a feature comedy or action-adventure about forty-five. Scene sequencers think in terms of crafting anywhere between six and twelve sequences, most often six to eight, in a feature story.

In an action story, sequences might start with a sequence in which the problem is presented, followed by a sequence where a team is assembled, followed by a sequence showing the team preparing and training for battle, followed by a sequence of traveling to the battle, followed by the battle sequence, and so on. Once scene sequencers have the sequences clearly defined, it's easier come up with the scenes necessary to complete each sequence. This concept is well described in *Screenplay: Writing the Picture*, by Robin U. Russin and William Missouri Downs. It is also covered in *Story*, by Robert McKee. Chris Soth teaches scene sequencing in *Million-Dollar Screenwriting: The Mini-Movie Method*, and Christopher Vogler explores myth structure using sequences of the "hero's journey" in his book *The Writer's Journey*.

THE ROADMAP APPROACH

The Roadmap approach breaks a story down into landmark events (plot points) that follow an established emotional journey. This approach might give the impression at first that it would produce boring stories, but that is true only if the writer has no imagination. Originality comes from the writer's ability to create unique content, context, and characters. If you think about the stories you have watched, read, or listened to, most of the stories you love the most probably follow a familiar plot. Yet you thoroughly enjoyed each incarnation of the plot pattern because of the writer's originality as to the world, themes, and characters of the story, as well as the story as a comment about the human condition and life in our society today. This is particularly true in myth stories that follow the hero's journey.

These familiar patterns work for love stories, action stories, and character stories alike. Following a roadmap approach can be a compelling way to tell a story because it forces you to follow a tried-and-true emotional journey.

To learn this approach, consider John Truby's seminars on his Twenty-two Building Blocks and Blake Snyder's book *Save the Cat!*

USING THEM ALL

When I approach a new idea, I have found great value in examining my story idea through the lens of several approaches. I'll start with a quick stab at Aristotle's beginning, middle, and end. A romp through the twelve-step hero's journey. A review of Egri's thoughts on unity of opposites, premise, character, and, specifically, the beginning and end emotional states of the characters. And perusing Linda Seger's wonderful collection of books for screenwriters.

Each pass brings up different considerations, and I don't immediately judge the value of any one thought. I just throw it down. Many of these ideas are ultimately thrown out, but some ideas that prove to be unusable frequently lead to other inspired ideas. This is my process. You find out what works best for you.

Chapter Three
TRAINING FOR SCREENWRITERS

There are four primary ways to learn how to write screenplays: attend class-based training (and write), read screenwriting how-to books (and write), ask a working screenwriter how to do it (and write), and figure it out on our own (and write). Below are some insights about the first three ways to learn. If you are a figure-it-out-as-you-go person, go for it. Just write!

COLLEGE DEGREE PROGRAMS

The high-profile Master of Fine Arts (MFA) in Screenwriting programs are at the University of California Los Angeles (UCLA), University of Southern California (USC), and New York University (NYU). There are other excellent programs, but these three are the toughest to get into, they have a very stringent vetting process, and have the greatest level of visibility and industry recognition. In addition, nearly every major university has a screenwriting program. In MFA programs, you will write screenplays and take critical studies courses in which you learn the history and art of film and, generally, produce small film projects. To select the best one for you, learn about the specifics of a program by searching the universities' websites.

The MFA programs at the top three schools are highly competitive. When I considered the UCLA program in the mid-'90s, the university was receiving 300 to more than 400 applications each year, to fill about fifteen to twenty-five slots. Today, the application numbers must be higher because of the greater visibility of screenwriting, its income potential and celebrity.

A secondary advantage of getting into an MFA program is that it can jumpstart your networking effort. Lew Hunter has oft told the story of a high-profile guest lecturer who offered an excellent piece of advice. In the Q&A after the lecture, one of the students asked if he could submit his script to him for consideration. The speaker's first response was that the student couldn't. Then he said that the student could by calling the speaker's assistant and explaining that he was at this talk and had permission to submit. The assistant would then provide a release, and the script could be submitted along with the signed release.

However, the speaker went on to explain that the student's submission would be a waste of effort. The speaker already had a well-established network of writers he turned to when he looked for a script to produce. So, there was no chance that the student's script would go anywhere with his company. The speaker went on to tell the group that the most important person in the room was not himself but the fellow students in the audience, because some of them would eventually become executives in the business. Nurturing those relationships would more likely lead to career openings than submitting a script to him. I believe USC students are told a similar story. One of the great advantages of MFA programs is the network of relationships you can develop with your peers.

That peer group has other advantages. After graduation, some students form personal writers' groups to continue the momentum of the MFA program and to motivate each other to keep writing. These groups usually meet weekly to read and discuss one another's writing and provide support.

The teachers in an MFA program are also invaluable assets. Agents, agencies, and networks regularly reach out to them to find the standout students—especially at the big three schools. If you get into one of these programs, respect and nurture relationships with your fellow students and teachers.

Finally, an MFA in Screenwriting might open the door to teaching.

CERTIFICATE PROGRAMS

Certificate programs also have a vetting process. Along with the application, writing samples are submitted. However, applicants for certificate programs face much less stringent scrutiny than MFA applicants. In this category are growing numbers of non-university-related film schools.

The UCLA Professional Program in Screenwriting started in 1995 as the result of faculty having to turn away hundreds of quality writers each year and wondering whether they could offer an alternative. That led to the certificate program, in which the focus is solely on writing screenplays—no critical studies element. Just know that these programs carry little weight when it comes to landing teaching or any other industry position. In the end, if you complete the coursework, you earn a certificate for your wall. The benefit is the pure focus on screenwriting.

For some, the certificate program works as a feeder to the MFA program. There is the potential to raise the level of your writing, build relationships with the teachers and, in some cases, get reference letters from staff. That might work in your favor when you apply or re-apply to the MFA program.

EXTENSION AND ADULT EDUCATION PROGRAMS

These programs are easy to get into. About the only pre-requisite is having the money and, in some cases, a modest writing sample. Early on, I took a couple of these programs and found that the students' writing experience varies, from people who have some screenwriting training and have written scripts or started scripts, to those who have little creative writing experience. If you are not up to applying to an MFA or Certificate program, this might be a perfect place to dip your toe in the water.

SEMINARS

There are teachers who travel the world and offer multiday training programs (usually, a weekend training). If you don't have the time to commit to a regular class, this is an excellent way to get focused training to start your education. And for those who are in or have completed classroom programs, these are a good way to add to your screenwriting education.

SCREENWRITING CONFERENCES

Screenwriting conferences are a weekend commitment. Most offer two days filled with thirty-minute and one-hour lectures and panels on focused subjects. In addition, most have a space for industry booths related to screenwriting—magazines, software companies, production companies, acting programs, screenwriting schools, etc. Some conferences also offer pitch fests—opportunities to pitch a script to agents or production companies. Typically, these give you the chance to present a five- to ten-minute pitch. Conferences are a great way to get a sense of the broader screenwriting and filmmaking community. You will also have the opportunity to mingle with hundreds of others on the screenwriting journey.

RETREATS

A fun way to advance your screenwriting education and experience is through screenwriting retreats. Some prominent teachers set up one- to two-week long screenwriting retreats, either to a convenient location for the teacher or to a fun vacation place. Each retreat is unique in what is covered. Vacation and writing in an exotic location. It doesn't get much better than that.

BOOKS

As noted, there is an abundance of screenwriting books on the market. Trying to choose a book to start with can be daunting. In the past two and a half decades, I've read more screenwriting books than I care to count, and I enjoyed them all. However, in screenwriting groups, there is constant discord over which is best to read first. A common thread starts when a new writer queries the community for a book recommendation and gets overwhelmed by the bickering that ensues among the group "experts." It's crazy and confusing.

In the long run, if you limit yourself to one book, you might be doing yourself a disservice. Professional writers are constantly learning new things and growing. You should, too.

DVD EXTRA FEATURES

Check the DVDs of your favorite movies for a writer, producer, or director voiceover track. You might pick up storytelling tips. *The Incredibles* has several bonus tracks well worth watching, that cover aspects of story and character development.

FELLOW SCREENWRITERS AND INDUSTRY PROFESSIONALS

There is great benefit to associating with writers and other industry people. Join writers' groups. Attend screenwriting networking sessions. Create a personal writers' group. Get your material out there, where it might be read. Get feedback. Discuss the art of screenwriting. Debate the subject. Be proactive and keep writing!

Chapter Four
DEVELOPING YOUR SCREENWRITING STYLE

This is a short chapter to touch on a subject rarely addressed. Style evolves through writing, reading, studying the art of writing, and making your own writing discoveries. Read screenplays, note what gets your attention, and try it out. Read as many produced screenplays as you can. I was a voracious reader and collector of feature scripts in my early days. I accumulated and read about a thousand scripts. All that reading significantly informed my writing style. However, the first noteworthy change to my writing style came after I completed a series of self-directed writing exercises.

As I was reading those thousand scripts, I wondered what it would be like to be in the room, looking over the shoulders of the top writers. Even better, what would it be like to know what they were thinking as they wrote? Then it occurred to me that I could simulate that by retyping script pages. So, I picked out about a dozen of my favorites, and I retyped the first five pages, word for word. Yes, it was overkill, but as a detail-minded person, I loved it.

Through this exercise, I picked up nuances that I incorporated into my style. Here's a excerpt from a script of mine, *Once a Spy*. I'm not implying that this is brilliant writing. It's not. I cite this only to show how I applied into my style what I gleaned from reading the great writers.

The scene is a military action sequence. A tactical unit is assaulting a farmhouse where bad guys have been reported to be holed up with biological weapons material.

INT. FARMHOUSE - HALLWAY - NIGHT

Soldiers flow down the hallway. Methodically. Quickly. No resistance as one by one, rooms are pronounced "Clear" until --

-- the last door. It's locked. A soldier SHOTGUNS a hole in the door and another tosses a concussion grenade through the opening. A beat later, BOOM. The men shoulder the door, but it barely moves because it's blocked by --

INT. FARMHOUSE - BACK ROOM - NIGHT

-- a stack of dead, bloated bodies.

In this sequence, I used style techniques from scripts written by David Koepp and by Ron Bass. David strategically breaks up certain paragraphs by using double hyphens in the middle of a sentence, creating a new paragraph starting with another set of double hyphens at the start of the remainder of the sentence. David's use of the double dashes brings focus to key action points. It also helps create more white space on the page. Other writers do the same thing using ellipses, but I prefer the look of the double dashes. From Ron Bass, I picked up his use of punchy one-word sentences.

Other writers use one-word sentences and dashes or hyphens to break up paragraphs, but I picked up these techniques from these two writers. Some techniques that work well for other writers didn't feel right for me. I tried and abandoned them.

Concerning marketability and writing a hit screenplay, years ago, I was struck by a talk given by cognitive psychologist and neuroscientist Daniel J. Levitin, PhD, author of *Your Brain on Music*. In a speech about songwriting, he said that "pleasurable music balances predictability with surprise, novelty with familiarity, [and] complexity with simplicity." He was talking about the common ingredients in hit songs, and his point goes to how the brain works.

Having read his book, my takeaway is that when something is novel, complex, and surprising, the brain's first response is to reject it—an auto-protect response that goes back to the early days of humankind, when anything out of the ordinary could mean danger and death. On the other hand, if something is predictable, familiar, and simple, the brain considers it no threat and ignores it. He noticed that hit songs universally balanced these two states. If you present a new song that has a level of comfort and familiarity, then the brain will be open to novel elements that might pique a listener's interest and excitement. The potential outcome is that the audience will want to hear the song over and over, and that is the hallmark of a hit.

Dr. Levitin's point resonated deeply with me, and I posit that this insight applies to all art, especially screenplays. If your stories are all about surprise, novelty, and complexity, you are likely to have a hard time finding many who will embrace them. Although some will love your work because it is extreme. Alternatively, if your stories are basically tried-and-true plots, they will probably bore people. The viewers will like them but not love them. Since listening to Dr. Levitin's talk, I noticed that movies that have a familiar foundational structure balanced with new, intriguing, and unexpected elements are the most successful. *Pirates of the Caribbean* is one such example. *The Matrix* is another. Both movies play on familiar plots but add unexpected twists to story and characters. Both movies also pushed the boundaries of CGI (computer-generated imagery) at the time—another unexpected element that piqued audiences.

Take these insights and develop your unique style.

Chapter Five
PRODUCTION DEVELOPMENT

This chapter lays out the path from pitch to production that feature film and network television production companies use to develop and produce projects. When I wrote a series of articles on development for *Script* magazine, I interviewed feature development execs and television development execs from a major studio and a mini-major studio about the development processes. This chapter pulls together what I learned from those interviews along with my own experience working in network television.

OVERVIEW

"Development" is a term used in both screenwriting and production. In writing, development loosely refers to the story development process of crafting, deepening, and enriching a story. This chapter is about production development: the process of acquiring stories and moving them to production. This process includes, among many other concerns, developing the script by providing notes to the writer(s) to hone the script to arrive at a pass that meets the needs of the production entity, identifying funding, and locking down contractual commitments from key personnel. Locking down talent is referred to as adding "attachments," for example attaching a director, actor, cinematographer, or producer to the project. Attaching talent is a tactic used in some instances to attract funding. On the feature film side of the business, development might involve a multiyear—sometimes multidecade—script rewriting process. On the other hand, in television, development happens quickly. There is a television year, and development happens or dies within that year.

Within feature development is "packaging." Packaging is a tactic to induce a studio to acquire a script. Major talent agencies will occasionally attach critical talent to a script—actors, directors, producers. These attachments are almost exclusively from that agency, and the agency pitches the package to a major or mini-major studio. They try to package a deal that studios can't refuse.

Today, companies like Netflix and Amazon broadcast original content. These content providers have opened more doors to new writers, and new territory for established writers to move into. However, as you venture into this world, know that if there is serious money available, you'll have serious competition, no matter where you turn. The reality in Hollywood is that there are far more writers fighting for positions than writing positions. The competition is brutal.

FEATURE FILM DEVELOPMENT

The feature world is composed of major studios (for example Paramount Pictures, Warner Bros., Walt Disney Studios, and Universal Studios), mini-major studios (for example Lionsgate, Artisan Entertainment, and Dimension Films), and countless independent production companies. Major and mini-major studios produce movies and television shows, and they own and run production lots with sound stages and outdoor sets. Independent production companies tend to be production companies only—basically, a shingle and office space. They don't own lots. When independents go into production, they rent production space from a major, mini-major, or independent studio facility (for example, Raleigh Studios, a production facility whose primary business is renting out its sound stages and other production services).

The primary difference among major, mini-major, and independent production companies lies in the number of movies they release each year and the size of their production budgets. Major studios release more than thirty films per year and are best known for big-budget blockbuster movies populated with A-list talent (writers, directors, and actors).

Mini-major studios generally release fewer than fifteen movies per year with smaller budgets, which means they must be frugal. Mini studios and independent production companies tend to make more cross-genre and experimental movies than major studios. If your script is a cross-genre or experimental script, don't expect to find much traction at a major studio.

While all productions want A-list talent, major studio projects depend on A-list talent. They need A-listers to realize the best vision of the story and to attract large audiences. Major studio budgets have grown to the point where they rely on revenue from worldwide audiences. Therefore, they need scripts that have broad demographic and cultural appeal.

To attract A-list talent, money is always a powerful inducement, but it's not always enough. A-list actors tend to seek roles that are different from what they have done before, roles that challenge them and have Oscar potential. A-list directors also look for projects with Oscar potential. They tend to attach to projects that inspire within them a clear vision for something that piques their passion. This is vital, because a major studio looks for a director with both a passion for the project and a clear vision for how to maximize the story elements (characters, settings, themes, in a comedy, knowing where the jokes will come from).

A-list talents can attach to a project for a variety of reasons: because they want to work with the studio, or to work with someone already attached, or as a quid pro quo. Actors might attach to a project they are not passionate about in exchange for the studio green-lighting a project the actor is passionate about but the studio is not. Studios might agree to this because they want to work with that actor. They want that relationship. Again, success in Hollywood is largely about building relationships at all levels.

Feature film production companies and feature divisions within a studio are constantly acquiring projects and moving them into development, without a set production start date. A story moves into development and remains there indefinitely (if the studio purchased the script and the necessary elements to get a greenlight are never met), until contractual options expire (in which case, the writer(s) get the rights back), or until enough elements come together to get the greenlight to move the project into production. Far more scripts move into feature development than ever get produced.

Feature development begins essentially when one of the following is purchased or optioned: a story pitch, spec script, rights to a book or short story, or rights to other source of a story idea (such as, a personal story that makes the news). Sometimes, production companies decide to remake a movie already produced and distributed the production company owns. In that event, the production company will move that project into development and hire a writer to come up with a fresh take on the movie.

Major studios are big machines, with a lot of bureaucracy. To get a green light, the writer and the project must successfully navigate the vagaries of the studio system. Even if a story gets purchased or optioned by a major studio, projects can be put on hold for myriad reasons. Two factors that cause delays between a script or story idea being purchased and a green light for production are the need to hone the story to meet the studio's stringent needs and waiting for matching windows to open in the schedules of multiple A-list talent (primarily actors, directors, and producers). Getting the key A-list talent pieces together in the same timeframe might be a significant challenge. To manage this, the studios track A-list commitments for five years or more.

Feature story development often means writing pass after pass to craft and polish the action, characters and themes. For the WGA writer, this might mean a steady income as he or she is tasked with rewrite after rewrite, or gets paid for option after option. The studio might also try a series of writers to find a vision of the story it wants to make.

The most maddening aspect of feature development is the time it takes for a project to creep through the system to get into production. Some projects have taken decades. The term "development hell" was coined to describe the way feature projects seem to simply churn and churn in development, striving towards the every-elusive green light that always appears to be far off. Politics can be never-ending, and just as a writer needs an insider champion to break into the industry, a story needs a development executive champion to keep senior execs focused on a project and keep it moving through the system.

PITCHING TO A FEATURE DEVELOPMENT EXECUTIVE

Pitching to a feature film development exec is similar to pitching to a television development exec. There's an initial five minutes of getting to know each other, followed by some fifteen minutes for the story pitch and answering questions. Many inexperienced writers hold to two ideas about feature pitching that are mistaken. First, they believe that as an unsold writer they can get a major studio pitch because their idea or script is just that brilliant and original. You're statistically never going to get a pitch meeting at a major studio if you are an unknown, especially if you're an unknown without an agent. (Although you might luck out and get a meeting if the right circumstances all come together perfectly.) Second, they believe that production companies take pitches to decide if they want to read a script. Production companies do not use pitches to decide if they want to read a script. They take pitch meetings to decide if they like a story concept enough to move it into development. If there is a script they have interest in, they will simply put that script into the reading pool for coverage (a report written by an assigned script reader who assesses the value of the script for that production company).

A final thought: should a production company accept your script and the development exec gives you notes, take those notes seriously. Do not expect a development exec to champion your script without his or her concerns being addressed. If you strongly disagree with the notes, you might win the argument, but if the exec does not feel confident promoting your script up the chain of command as is, your script might never get out of his or her office.

TELEVISION DEVELOPMENT

To do this justice, this section would be a very lengthy and complicated discussion. However, I will simply walk you through a cursory overview of the players and the activity.

Television writing started with the big three networks: ABC, CBS, and NBC. Today, the television world is vast. The big three are still the money giants, but might not be for long. In network television, there is a distinct network television year. Not all the other venues for television content are tied to this network television year. If your dream is to work in primetime, network television, it helps to understand this when you plan your breaking-into-television-writing strategy—such as, sending out script samples, looking for an agent, pitching, and so on. It would be a waste of time to try to get a network pitch meeting during a time of the year when no one in network television is taking pitches, such as, during pilot season (January through April).

This network television year begins and ends with the Network Upfronts in mid-May. This is when the major networks announce their fall lineup to advertisers and to the world, with a lot of fanfare. It's a formal, staged presentation that generally includes the executive producer(s) and principal cast. The Upfronts are also when the studios learn which of their pilots have been picked up—that is, ordered into production—as well as which of their existing shows are either coming back or being cancelled. For shows returning, May is the time they have fulfilled their delivery obligation of episodes for the previous season, and the show is in hiatus. For the writing-producing staff of a show coming back, this down time lasts about a month or so before they come back.

Intuitively, you might think that the network year would begin and end with the start of a new season in September. It's not a September-to-September cycle because television productions need several months to hire a full writing-producing staff, plan the season arc, write the first few script, and begin production so that in September, there are shows in the can to air.

For television series, it's the business affairs department that negotiates the deals for series staff writers, producers (most are writer-producers but there are some pure producers), principal actors as well as the episodic writers and directors. Business affairs also negotiates hundreds of "If-come" deals (deals made after a pitch in which no money is paid to the writer unless the project is sold). Most if-come deals coming out of a pitch are are a commitment for that season only. Producers and writer-producers on staff are hired for multiple seasons in which the studio has the option to pick them up season after season, or not. After the Upfronts, the network television business affairs departments send the previous year's unfunded if-come deals to the archives, and starts all over. It's a clean slate coming into June. Each season, if I recall correctly, it's typical for each business affairs executive to negotiate or have active files on some 100 comedy and 100 drama development deals each year. Some projects from a previous year do carry forward, but that requires negotiating a new if-come deal.

Within the network television year, the series television shows have distinct seasons and the studio has different distinct seasons. On the series production track, there is staffing season (when they hire the staff of writer-producers), planning the season's writing (working out the season's broad story arc), then writing the scripts and producing episodes. On the studio side, there is pitching season, pilot-writing season and pilot-production season—and these seasons overlap. For this discussion, there are three key studio department: business affairs, legal and development. It's the job of the studio's development department to find series concepts, miniseries, and television movie ideas to pitch to the networks.

In television series production, writers are also producers. Managing is part of the job, and immediately after the Upfronts, television staffing season begins. This is when writing staffs are locked down. The returning writers are simply picked up for that season, but it's standard to add or replace some staff members. The last writing position to be filled is generally the entry-level staff writer. If the entry-level staff writer from the previous season is picked up, he or she automatically advances to the position of story editor, leaving a vacancy for a new entry-level writer. Television writing is one arena where they choose you because of your initial writing talent but they expect you to learn writing-producing on the job. One other note, in the television world, the writer-producer calls the shots, and the directors take orders from the writer-producer. In the feature film world, the director calls the shots.

For those wanting to pursue a career as a television writer, here are some insights about the competition. Most writing staffs have six to twelve writer-producers, with one, at best, two of them being the entry-level staff writer position that season. Each writer-producer has an agent with a crop of new writers looking for a seat. That's six to twelve agents with direct influence potentially submitting a writer for the entry-level chair next season. Outside of that, studios and the networks routinely look for new writing talent and groom them for a seat on one of their shows. That's another couple handfuls of political, high-level submissions. Then there's the crop of writers from agents who do not have someone on staff but who have industry influence. Then there is the world of non-connected writers desiring a shot. All these people are jockeying for one or two openings. This is how competitive landing a staff writing job is today.

Pilot-pitching season begins in earnest a few weeks after the Upfronts and ends when the last pilot script writing order is given out, generally in the October-November timeframe. The bulk of pitches happen between June and September, and the season basically ends when the networks and studios have spent their pilot writing budgets. Each year, networks set a budget for funding pilot writing. When that pot is exhausted, they basically stop taking series pitches.

After the Upfronts, most of the major television network development execs in town take vacations. When they return, one of their first actions is to hold meetings to decide what kinds of pitches they want and do not want to see that season. Much of this decision making is based upon research into trends. The networks then pass that information on to the studios and agencies, who, in turn, reach out to their writers who were not placed on staff so they can start working up concepts to pitch.

During pitching season, the typical pitching process begins when an agent contacts the studio development departments with ideas he or she wants his or her writer to pitch to the studio. The development execs take pitch meetings and decide which ones to lock down. To lock down a pitch, the development exec tasks the business affairs department to make a deal. A business affairs exec will then contact the writer's representative and negotiate an "if-come" deal.

In business affairs, the 100 new drama development projects and 100 new comedy development projects negotiated each year that I referenced earlier was the workload for just one of five business affairs executives. This gives you some perspective on the number of projects that one major studio negotiates each year and the number of pitches that go on.

When an if-come deal is negotiated, it's a win-win for the writer and the studio. It doesn't cost the studios anything upfront to make a deal, and the writer get a champion for their idea. Projects pitched are, in general, story ideas for television series, miniseries, and television movie concepts. Occasionally, the rights to a book will be negotiated in anticipation that it might be right for conversion to one of these formats.

Once a deal is in place, the next step is for the development exec to work with the writer to polish a pitch to take to the network. Once the network pitch is polished, the development exec sets up a pitch meeting with the network development execs.

Pilot writing season officially begins when the studio gets the first pilot writing commitment. As an aside, studios or production companies will occasionally pay a writer to write a pilot script when there is a project they believe strongly in that has not received a network order. But this very rare. I recall only a couple in the twelve years that I worked in business affairs and legal.

Pilot production season starts in January and finishes by the end of April. Drama pilots generally are the first to be produced because they take the longest to shoot and edit. They tend to have many locations, have tedious action sequences to shoot and a longer editing process than comedies. Traditional comedies are shot on a sound stage in front of a live audience, and the scripting, shooting and editing happen much more quickly. Therefore, comedies tend to be shot later in pilot season.

THE BASIC DYNAMICS OF TELEVISION REVENUE

There are two primary, underlying revenue streams in network television: advertising revenue for networks and license fees for studios. Studios invest money to produce content for television and then charge a broadcast license fees to the network for the right to broadcast that content for a specified period of time. Over time, studios generate increased revenue by repeatedly licensing content. There are other revenue streams for studios, such as DVD sales, but this studio-network relationship is the foundation of the business.

Networks generate revenue through the sale of commercial time, and the advertising cost is dependent on time slots and the audience that tunes in. Not all audiences are highly valued. In general, older audiences are easier to reach and thus less valuable. Younger audiences are traditionally the hardest to reach and the most desired. Ideally, the network wants a series so hot that there is a bidding war for commercial time. When the networks are unable to get sufficient revenue from their commercial time slots, they tend to dump the show. This is why your favorite show might have been canceled, even though it was a hit with critics.

There is financial jeopardy for both studios and networks. If it turns out commercial time cannot be sold for what the network expects to generate, the network will fail to bring in enough revenue to justify the license fee. If that is the case, the natural response is to cancel the series and pay the studio the penalty for pulling the plug. Part of most series negotiations is an order for a minimum number of guaranteed episodes with an option for a back-end pickup for more. For example, the negotiations might be for a thirteen-episode guarantee with a back-end pickup of eleven more episodes, for a total of twenty-four episodes in a season. If a series is cancelled, say, three or four episodes into the season, the network owes the studio the fees for the full initial order.

For the studios, the cost of production is far greater than the license fees and foreign distribution fees they receive for the initial airing. To make a profit, they look to produce enough episodes so that they have a block to continually relicense. Over time, a hit can pay for many failures. This dynamic keeps the studios in business.

To get a sense of the monies studios deficit spend each season, here is a simple example of what might happen to a drama series. It's not uncommon for a network television drama to cost upwards of $3.5 million per episode to produce—and this is on the low end. Given a twenty-four-episode order, the studio might have to deficit finance (or go out of pocket) more than $50 million per year after license fees and foreign distribution. This is probably on the low end. The studios lose money on the first runs betting that they will make money in the long run by producing enough episodes to package and continually licensing reruns. In years past, the goal was to reach 100 episodes to form a package.

TELEVISION PITCHING

Major studio pitch meetings are initiated almost exclusively by agents. There might be exceptions, involving meetings being set up from outside the world of agents, but the exceptions are extremely few. My meetings with Paramount execs were set without an agent because I worked there. Over the years, I booked two feature development pitch meetings and two television development pitch meetings. One feature meeting was the result of a fortuitous encounter with a feature producer on the lot. The other feature meeting was a proposed co-writing effort with an experienced WGA writer I got to know. That meeting was set up through his agent.

A typical television pitch runs about twenty minutes. If the execs like what they are hearing and want to know more, the pitch might stretch to forty minutes. It's pretty much the same as a feature pitch meeting, the first five minutes are social—a meet-and-greet for everyone to get comfortable with each other. After that, the next five minutes are the most critical. Within five minutes of launching into the pitch, the television exec will usually have made up his or her mind about it. So, the time to grab their interest is right up front. In the following fifteen minutes, the writer will need to express succinctly the who, what, when, where, and why of the story concept. Many execs will want to know how the writer came up with the idea. Those execs believe that a project based upon something personal to the writer are the most successful. They believe the writer's personal connection to the story engages an audience more profoundly.

One piece of advice that I got from more than one exec is to pitch passionately and in an interesting way. Tell the execs what you want to do, a little bit about where the idea came from, the central characters, and what a couple of episodes might be. Two common pitching mistakes are to pitch a concept that is little more than a version of something already on the market and successful or to pitch a project like one that aired and failed.

One final reality regarding television pitching: without credibility as a writer—especially as a television writer—you are not likely to get anywhere. And, if you do wrangle a pitch as an unproduced television writer, don't be surprised if the execs basically shine you on. The experience of the writer is as important, if not more important, to the pitch as the project. For the studio and the network, the critical position is the Executive Producer, Showrunner. Someone who has a proven track record of pulling together a quality staff and turning out twenty-four episodes each season on time, on budget, that catch and hold an audience they want to advertise to. The studios and the networks are more interested in being in business with the proven writer-producer than the series concept. So, don't beat yourself up or put undue attention on getting the chance to pitch early in your drive to launch a television writing career. First, work to get on staff.

GETTING A PILOT SCRIPT WRITING GREEN LIGHT AND NOTES

Given that networks have limited pilot writing budgets each season, exceedingly few network pitches lead to a green light to write a pilot. When a pilot script is ordered, the writing goes through the development process of writing a treatment, an outline, and finally the script. At each step, the writer must address both studio and network notes. The studio development exec shepherds this writing process and will not send a treatment, outline, or script to the network until the studio and network notes are properly addressed. In this process, it's vital that the writer develop a very good relationship with the execs.

Chapter Six
BASIC HOLLYWOOD POLITICS

This chapter provides a broad-brushstroke look at the lay of the political land. The point of this chapter is to provide a foundational understanding of the competing forces within the industry. It would take several books to truly capture the essence of Hollywood politics. The intent here is to give you a sense of the political dynamics in play.

LONGEVITY IN THE BUSINESS

Longevity in this industry is tied to a host of factors. Primary among them is one's ability to work well with others and to deliver consistent, professional results. Despite what you might think, not everyone with longevity is brilliant at their work. Most deliver yeoman's work effort. Brilliant execution is always desired, but not if that brilliance is hit or miss or takes too long to deliver. Quality, dependable work wins out in the long run. Many writers who work regularly do so because they fit in well and deliver solid, dependable work quickly. In television, quality work done quickly is highly valued over slow brilliance. Television is very fast paced. Maybe the analogy is that television is about sprinters and features are about long-distance runners.

As a new person, you represent an unknown quantity and might have too many potential failings to risk hiring. Projects must keep moving smoothly through a rigorous production timeline to be profitable. The mantra in the industry is to deliver on time and on budget. If someone slows up work or causes extensive delays for any reason, the result might be that the production runs late and over budget. That might affect a lot of people negatively and reduce the production company's profits.

Dependability is what drives production companies to go from project to project using much of the same, trusted production team. If you are new, fighting to break in and feel your talents are exceptional, you might wonder, "Why don't they trade out okay talent for better talent? Like me." This comes back to the edict to deliver product on time, on budget. As an unknown, it might be difficult to find someone willing to take the risk that you might not perform effectively on a production.

This especially applies to writers in television. The pressure on a writing staff to turn out quality product week-to-week for a full season is high. Any delay has significant ripple effects. You've probably noticed when, in the middle of a season, suddenly your favorite television show runs one or two reruns instead of new episodes. This is probably because something, or someone, caused the writing or production chain to back up. As a result, the show was unable to deliver the next episode or episodes on time for broadcast. That's why it's so hard to break in; the unknown person might be good or might be bad for the production, and that's a coin the industry doesn't like to toss.

There are many hurtles a television script must go through to be produced and air. The story must be approved by the showrunner or the head of the writing staff as well as the studio and the network. Any one of these three can shoot down a pitch. After a story pitch is accepted, a treatment is written and must be approved by all three. Then an outline and finally the script. Along the way, all notes at each level must be addressed. As the story goes through the writing process, legal will review every story for rights approvals and the like. A budget is put together and challenged. Some scenes or location may be financially impossible to use. The approval process can be arduous. And these are just some of the challenges the writer and the show faces.

Hopefully, you are beginning to see why producers tend to hire the same people over and over. Once they find someone who can fill the bill, the producer can focus on other challenges. They hang on to people they come to trust to deliver quality work product and whom they also come enjoy or at least get along with on a daily basis. Production hours commonly run twelve or more hours per day, sometimes including weekend days. That much time working side-by-side, under pressure, necessitates working with people you get along with. Imagine spending that much time together daily with someone you don't like. Tension would naturally build up and boil over. Even with a team that is like a tight-knit family, production offices and sets will get emotionally heated from time to time because of pressure and proximity. That's a given. Mitigating that is vital.

Longevity can also be tied to the success of the projects worked on. Those with long careers tend to have achieved that status because of the above and probably because the projects they have worked on were successful—either making money or garnering awards. The award(s) might not be directly attributable to that person, but he or she reaps the benefits. Successful projects bring attention to all who work on the projects.

Since a financially successful project raises the visibility of nearly everyone involved, some people on a project, at some emotional level, might feel that their careers are on thin ice and be wary of rookies. I'm being a bit over dramatic on this point, but there is an underlying validity to this concern. If an unknown talent is hired, believe me, people are watching. And in some cases, if that person can't deliver properly and quickly, people will voice concern and the production might fire that person.

Since many in the industry typically work from production to production, many are simultaneously looking for their next job while working the current one. If a project runs long, that might result in some involved in the production missing the start of the next project and cause them to lose that opportunity and income. This is another reason industry people might be leery of a new person.

Word of mouth travels fast. Production time is expensive, and if you cause a production to go over budget, the word will get around. A feature film production (and television shows) can easily employ over a hundred people. When production is held up, the hourly rate of all the people being held up is significant. While expense for delays is calculated into the budget, too many delays will lead to cost overruns.

From a writer's perspective, your inability to deliver a quality product on time during production is critical. For example, say a production company buys your script and pays you to address notes. You work hard, and after several rewrites the script is in such good shape that the project goes into production, that's not the end of your writing duties. All along the production timeline, you will constantly have notes to address. Many of the rewrites will be the result of production issues. Take the example of an actor being cast who doesn't precisely fit the character as written. That might require a rewrite to accommodate that actor. Or say a location the script calls for is not available, or, if late in the production, that location is then too expensive because of cost overruns. That will require a rewrite for a different, often less-expensive location. Any number of issues can force rewrites as the production is shooting. As the writer, it's your job to handle the ever-changing writing demands of production, and to do your job quickly and effectively.

Imagine the cost of a delay in production if you are slow on the rewrites or if your rewrites are deemed unacceptable. They can't shoot without script pages. If your inability becomes enough of a liability, the production company might be forced to fire you and bring on a new writer. If they replace you and go over budget because of the delay, imagine the impact. Think of the ripple effect your failure might have on other key people on the project, those whose next job is potentially tied to the success of their current job and the job ending on time. In Hollywood, positive and negative word spreads instantaneously, and negative outcomes spread the fastest and can kill a career. That's why the industry often seems to live by the rule, "The devil you know is better than the devil you don't." Respect this.

If you get an opportunity to work in the business, be a team player and be respectful of situations and people.

HOLLYWOOD IS A BUSINESS AND BEAN COUNTERS RULE THE ROOST

Script-purchase decisions are, obviously, directly tied to potential profitability. What you might not know is that somewhere in the script-purchasing pipeline, there is an analyst accountant who estimates potential revenue. Analysts consider demographics, regional expectations, international expectations, and much more. For the major studios, it's a worldwide market. This means a big-budget script must appeal to many cultures to be sufficiently profitable. If the analyst calculates that there isn't enough profit in your script as is, a script sale is pretty much a bust. Consequently, it might feel like the bean counters rule the roost.

Certainly, many other considerations are involved in a script sale, but few get purchased if there is no potential profit in it. This is one reason scripts get rewritten to death. For example, a bean counter might have concluded that adding a love-story element to an action story will bring girlfriends to the theaters along with the men and make enough of a revenue difference to be potentially profitable. Similarly, they might conclude that adding an action element to a love-story element will bring in boyfriends, or that adding some other element will bring in some other significant demographic (e.g., teen girls, teen boys, parents and children). These types of considerations are just some of the behind-the-scenes politics that come into play, because Hollywood is a business.

Everyone I know has left a movie theater at least one time wondering why something so convoluted was made. Now you can blame the bean counters and not the writers.

THE POLITICS OF RECEIVING STORY AND SCRIPT NOTES

One of the most emotionally crushing frustrations beginning writers universally face is handling notes. All writers face notes, but first-time writers tend to fiercely resist criticism. Part of being a professional writer is your ability to receive and professionally act upon notes. When addressing notes, there will be times when you should stand up for your choices and engage in a healthy debate, but there are times when you just need to close your trap and listen. Then deliver. When you listen, do so with an open mind. Most of the time, there will be a healthy dialog to go along with notes.

For blockbuster movies, dialogue must cross cultural lines, and some American cultural idioms do not translate. When I was in Turkey, one of the Turks said to me, "The road is like a pill." Confused, I asked what that meant. He explained that it meant that the road was very narrow, like a pill is narrow. That saying doesn't exist in American culture. If that had been a line in a movie, I might have not understood what was meant and missed the next three speeches wondering what a road "like a pill" meant. If there is too much of that kind of confusion, you can lose a foreign audience completely. If you've ever wondered why the dialogue in action movies is so simplistic, this might be the answer.

I gained useful notes-receiving experience while going through the UCLA writing programs. However, I gained my next most valuable experience when I joined a professional writers' group. One writers' group I was a part of (which is still going strong) is predominantly composed of working writers, directors, producers, and SAG actors. Each week, four writers present thirty minutes of material, followed by fifteen minutes of comments. If the material is a screenplay or a play, the writer brings enough sides (script pages) to cast the acting parts with the actors in the room, plus a side for the narrator to read everything that is not dialogue. After the read, the actors return to their seats, and the writer and moderator take the stage to listen to comments and questions from the group. The operative word is listen.

My first time in the hot seat was brutal emotionally. The group gave me great marks for story, but some of my darlings, my favorite scenes or favorite elements within a scene, were universally criticized—a dagger to the heart. At first, the negative comments felt like a politely disguised way of saying that I sucked as a writer. I was defensive and argumentative, but each time I tried to push back, the moderator gently cut me off and politely informed me that the fifteen minutes is for the group to comment and for me to listen and answer questions. The third time up, I was finally calm and confident enough to let my guard down, and I discovered that getting notes was quite liberating.

I discovered that when my darlings were hated, it was usually because I had failed to get across effectively what was in my head. In some cases, the scenes or scene elements had to be cut, but in most cases, I simply had to rewrite to make my thoughts clear. I learned that a note was not a critique of my writing skill. It was a suggestion for improvement.

If your script gets into development—meaning your script has been purchased—inevitably, the production company will require changes. At this point, the company owns the script, and, after that, you are effectively hired help. If they hire you to do rewrites, which they normally do, you must do what they want or they will bring on a new writer. They might direct you to cut scenes you might not want to cut or add scenes and elements you don't want to add. This does not mean you won't have substantive dialogues with the development exec. You will. This is just to make the point that, after the script is purchased, you alone cannot make decisions on changes to the script. You will have to get good at receiving and addressing notes.

Here's another personal experience regarding notes, my most significant experience. I had an action script optioned in the late '90s. The budget was set at a modest $25 million. A director was quickly attached. That first week, the trade magazines picked up the story, and the script, the production company, the director and I were mentioned—thrilling for a first-time writer.

During my first meeting with the director, he gave me incredible notes for a quick rewrite. Later, he instructed me to cut fifteen critical pages out of the middle of the script and replace them with a chase sequence. That scared the hell out of me. I was given the weekend to complete that. The changes significantly altered my carefully structured story, but I had no choice. He later instructed other significant scene changes and admitted that some of the big rewrites were because he wanted to shoot those scenes for his reel (a reel being a collection of scenes he has directed to showcase his talents). In this case, he was using my script to advance his career toward the big-budget feature arena. It was my job to make the changes and have them work organically with the story.

In the end, dealing with his notes and the rewriting was a challenge, but I agreed with most of his notes and they made the story stronger. It was an enlightening and wonderful experience.

CAPTAINING YOUR SCRIPT SHIP

Here is an analogy concerning notes that I found useful. Think of yourself as the captain of your ship—a script ship. On a ship at sea, the captain's primary job is to get the ship to the appropriate port. The passengers or the crew might want to go to Hawaii, but if the ship's scheduled destination is San

Diego, the captain must make all the course corrections to get the ship to San Diego. When you put your script out for comments, you will get opinions about other potential ports that readers think would be the best destination. If you make script changes based on notes everyone gives you, your story is likely to fall apart because it will not be of one mind.

Until a production company purchases your script and gives you notes that you can't ignore, notes are opinions. You decide which are valid or not. Ultimately, you are the captain of your spec script, and you need to make sure it gets to the port you intend to reach. Take in notes, but keep your story of one mind. When I provide notes to a writer, I tell them that the notes are my opinions based on my sensibilities, and if he or she finds that ten percent of my comments helps improve the script, I'm happy. When I provide notes, I don't take ownership of whether they are acted upon or not. Neither should you. When you are asked to read a script and offer your thoughts, do so sincerely and let the writer decide if your thoughts improve the script or not. You should accept notes in the same manner.

Chapter Seven

NETWORKING

For some writers, the thought of networking—meeting, greeting, and developing relationships with people who might advance their career or not—can turn an otherwise confident writer into a sweating mass of fear and doubt. Yet, networking is a necessary skill set, and, yes, it is a skill set. If you struggle with this, develop your people skills and learn to be proficient just as you would learn to be proficient at anything else: Be proactive. Read people-skills books. Find a friend who is expert at networking and have a conversation about how he or she approaches meeting strangers and building relationships. Learn to be a good conversationalist. Learn to be a good listener. Get out there and mingle. Try, fail, adjust and repeat.

Here are some networking opportunities about breaking into the industry—not all necessarily about breaking in as a writer:

FIGURE OUT WHERE INDUSTRY PEOPLE HANG OUT, AND HANG OUT THERE

When a writing friend of mine moved to Hollywood to launch his career, he was confident that bars would be an opportune place to meet industry people socially. He also assumed that establishments near the studios would be the best logical place to start. It wasn't long before he identified a promising location and became a regular.

Week after week, he made new friends and built relationships. That eventually led to an industry job at a major studio. Once inside, he developed new contacts on the lot. The contacts he made led to a creative position with a production company. That work led to his break as a writer. Today, because of his networking efforts and writing skills, he is a Writers Guild of America, West member. Without his dedication to proactive networking efforts, he might still be trying to get a break.

TAKE A JOB IN A STUDIO MAILROOM

Each studio has a mailroom, and it's possible to apply for a mailroom job off the street. This is a tried-and-true path to landing an industry job—although not necessarily a writing job. Once on the lot, schlepping mail around, you will meet people—mostly assistants, but execs, other key players and people at on-lot independent production companies as well. Be sociable, not needy, clingy or fawning.

When I worked at Paramount Pictures, quite a few mailroom personnel who serviced our offices came and went. They were all hardworking and social, but there was a regular turnover as they moved on to more appealing gigs. It works. This is one way to get inside.

ATTEND INDUSTRY FUNCTIONS

If you are near one of the three major industry hubs—Los Angeles, New York City, or Atlanta—look for industry functions (screenings, wrap parties, special event parties at a studio or production company, sporting events attended by industry people). Do your homework, and keep at it. You can find events to attend. Work to get into events where you are the least successful and least experienced. Network up. Then get good at meeting people and starting engaging conversations.

ATTEND WRITERS' GROUP MEETINGS

Generally, writers' groups allow people to audit for free. Look for local writers' groups. They're not hard to find. To become a member, there usually is a monthly fee, and some require writing samples to be reviewed before acceptance. One of the advantages of joining a writers' group is being able to associate with its members, who can offer a wealth of information and contacts. Most writers readily share what they have learned. An additional value of attending writers' group meetings is the chance to meet guest speakers, who tend to be working writers, agents, and producers. After a guest speaker's presentation, the speaker often hangs out and mingles. Sometimes, if the speaker is an agent or a producer, these encounters can lead to permission to submit a script to the agent or production company.

WORK ON SMALL PRODUCTIONS

Many regularly-working industry people also work on small projects from time to time, either as a favor for a friend or to gain experience outside of their main talent for their résumé. For example, a working writer might want directing experience and write a low-budget project to direct. He or she might even fund it and attract other people to help, either for the cross-field experience or as a favor. Low-budget projects and shorts are constantly being produced, and they need people willing to work in many capacities for little or no money. One way to make new contacts is to volunteer for such projects.

WORK ON FILM SCHOOL PROJECTS

Universities' film programs and independent film schools regularly need actors and other production help from outside of their programs. This work is typically unpaid. Again, you work on these projects to gain experience and meet people. You never know where the contacts will lead.

NETWORK THROUGH SCREENWRITING CLASSES

The title says it all. As I pointed out about the networking benefits of an MFA program, there are basic adult education screenwriting classes at about every major university that might provide networking opportunities as well. The courses are relatively inexpensive, and you never know who you will meet who might lead you to a high-value contact. The teacher might have valuable contacts and be willing to share.

USE A UNIQUE SKILL OR TALENT TO NETWORK

Leverage a unique skill or background to land industry work or a meeting. My Navy SEAL background led to work as a technical consultant and acting. Do you have a special skill, talent or experience that can open doors? If so, brainstorm ways your experience can be useful to someone in the industry, and reach out.

IN GENERAL, BE CREATIVE AND OPEN TO OPPORTUNITIES

Keep your mind open to opportunities. Attending my first UCLA Writers Block party—formerly, a monthly gathering for writers in UCLA programs, hosted by Lew Hunter—I read through a pile of old screenwriting MFA student newsletters laid out on his coffee table. After reading them all, I asked Lew how I could get on the mailing list. He told me the newsletter was out of print. That struck me as odd. How could it be that no student in the program recognized the newsletter as a vehicle to be able to interview some of the top talent in town and thereby get a chance to network at the highest levels—all under the prestigious banner of UCLA? Really? No one in the program thought of that?

Later that night, I asked for and was given permission to resurrect the newsletter. Under the UCLA MFA banner, I did interview top agents, actors, writers, show runners, producers and studio executives. No door seemed to be closed to me when I asked for an interview. The interviews allowed me to ask questions I wanted to know. More important, I developed relationships—especially with Lew and Pamela Hunter. Years later, writing that newsletter led to my book, *The Screenwriting Life*, published by Penguin Putnam's Berkley Boulevard Books. It also led to a senior writer gig for *Script* magazine and opened other industry doors.

Get out there, and get involved. Keep your mind open. Sharpen your people skills. If you work at networking, and you have something of value, you will find opportunities.

Chapter Eight
GOAL SETTING AND SUCCESSFUL WRITING HABITS FOR SCREENWRITERS

Goal setting is fundamental to success in every field. If you are not properly setting and accomplishing goals, then you are relying on luck to realize your dreams.

Goal setting is built on two pillars: dreams and goals. Some think these are the same thing, but there is an important functional difference between the two. The dream is the engine—the motivational element. Goals are the actions necessary to accomplish the dream. For a dream to be the most effective, it absolutely must be a burning desire. For a goal to be effective, it must be an action you alone are in total control of accomplishing, and it must have a completion date. The date element is important for discipline and continuity of effort. If you don't force yourself to complete goals by a specified date, you will very likely drag the process on longer than necessary or never reach your dream.

Come to appreciate the effect dreams and goals have on accomplishment. And keep in mind that every goal must be totally up to you to accomplish. It's not a goal if someone else must act for it to be completed. As a screenwriter, you might want to be paid a million dollars for a script. That would be a dream and not a goal because being paid a million dollars is not in your control. Someone other than you must pay that million dollars. Maybe that payday motivates you to write consistently, that would be a valuable dream. Then focus on the goals that might get you that payday.

The first step in this process is to identify your dream. Ask yourself, what is so deeply important to you that it will keep you steadfastly working to accomplish the often-tedious goals necessary to realize that dream? Find that singleness of purpose. Once you have identified your dream, divide accomplishing that dream into all the elements required to achieve it. Plot those goals onto a timeline, and commit to methodically accomplishing each goal. If the goal is big, break it down into smaller, more manageable goals.

For screenwriters, honing all the skills necessary to continually turn out professional scripts might take writing as many as a dozen scripts. Some writers will hit a home run within their first couple of scripts, but for most, it will take a many more attempts to hone the skill sets. Put this into your expectations and plan accordingly. Setting unreasonable expectations can cause you to back off on the continuity of effort that is necessary to achieve your desired end, especially when you don't see progress. To become a paid screenwriter, three things are critical: writing scripts, developing relationships (networking), and timing (having just the right script when you meet a just the right contact who is looking for such a script). It pretty much takes all three.

Above all, consider setting a goal of a daily writing habit. In setting this goal, maybe your available daily time slots are limited and not ideal for when you write best. Even though the time slots are not ideal, choose the most effective slot available and commit to it. Maybe in the beginning your ability to maintain focus fades quickly. Give yourself time to grow your ability to focus longer. Set a duration you can commit to keeping. If, say, your mind wanders after fifteen minutes of concentrated writing effort, start with twenty minutes as your daily habit. Push yourself. Fight your comfort zone when setting this goal and other goals. Discipline and stretching oneself is one of the foundational elements of success. Then, as you develop a greater capacity to work, increase your commitment.

After you set a time commitment goal, set a regular time of day for your writing routine. Nearly every professional screenwriter I have interviewed has expressed an awareness of when he or she is most creative, and writes during that period of peak creativity. It's a fixed time and duration. If your peak period of creativity is not a time when it's practical to write, pick the best time to write, given your restrictions. Figuring this out might take trial and error.

Most professionals write about four hours a day, at the same time each day. This is the foundation of their financial and career accomplishments. It's a habit. However, most launched their writing careers by first carving thirty to sixty minutes of writing time out of their sleep time and organize the rest of their life around this commitment. Most got up an hour early, feeling that their mind was clearer first thing in the morning than late at night. At first, this commitment was a challenge, but over time it became a habit and led to turning out product. That eventually led to a screenwriting career.

Setting screenwriting goals begins with the steps required to write a script: come up with a story idea, then flesh that out into a treatment, followed by an outline, a first-draft screenplay, and then polishing the screenplay. This is the pattern taught in the UCLA Professional Program in Screenwriting and the master's program in screenwriting.

You can also set goals for networking. The screenwriting community is large and a great place to develop contacts, learn about screenwriting, and gather insights about the industry. You'll also find the community is very supportive of one another.

Overall, be active. Meet and greet. Go online to screenwriting community sites. Check out links and other areas of advice they provide. Peruse the Writers Guild of America site—it's massive. Join social screenwriting networks. If your people skills are weak, again, read books on the subject and force yourself to go out and practice. This is a skill that you should learn to do well. Remember, Hollywood is an industry where people avoid working with people they don't like. Don't be one of those people.

When you plan your calendar, consider setting writing, training and networking goals. Successful people live by the mantra of try, fail, adjust, repeat. Live by this philosophy.

Examples of some goals you can set:

- Develop a daily writing habit. It's best to set it at the same time each day. As an aside, Lew Hunter recommended to me that when you sit down to write script pages, plan to turn out about ten script pages a day and to stop in the middle of a scene. Before you start into new pages, begin by doing some minor rewriting of the previous day's effort. This will help you get the creative juices flowing. When you reach the end of the previous day's pages, you are in the middle of a scene that has inherent energy and momentum. This advice has been a godsend to me.

- Read scripts on a regular basis. I read daily. For example, commit to reading for fifteen minutes every day.

- Research books on screenwriting to study, decide which appeal to you the most, and purchase them. Read them. Underline. I regularly go back to the books in my library to review, reread or at least look at my underlines and notes.

- Set out time for ongoing education. Research screenwriting classes. There are online and in-class opportunities. Get into a screenwriting class. Attend and complete all assignments.

- Develop your dialogue skills by actively listening to people talk. Get out and listen. Note speech patterns and accents so that you can duplicate the rhythms in your writing. Notice how a non-native English speaker formulates sentences. Notice the speech patterns that various cultures use when speaking English. A person from Europe speaking English has a distinct speech pattern that is different from a person from Asia. You can also observe this by watching television or YouTube.

- Commit time to researching networking opportunities, such as finding out about and attending film festivals, screenwriting conferences, and other industry events. Participate in every practical way you can.

- Join a writers' group. Members will be a wonderful source of industry contacts and writing insights.

- Create or join a private writers' group. No more than four to five other writers at your level or slightly above who are committed to meeting weekly to read and offer comment on one another's work. If you are not in a major city, try online screenwriting groups as a source.

- Submit to competitions. Work backwards from the submission date to establish the goals necessary to complete your writing by the submission date.

- Take an acting class to better understand the actor's process.

Chapter Nine
SUPPORT COMMUNITIES

There is an abundance of writing support communities. The Internet is thick with online screenwriters' groups, and most have a wealth of free screenwriting information.

The Writers Guild of America website (www.wga.org) is packed with information. If you navigate to the WGA's Writers' Room, among other places to explore on the site, you'll find screenwriting-themed articles, podcasts and links to interview videos. On the site, you'll also have access to everything you want to know about contracts and wages.

Check out your local community. Your local university will likely have screenwriting adult education, undergraduate classes and a master's program. Connect with screenwriters locally. Again, consider forming a personal writers' group of four to six people. Any more than six, and you will have too many opinions and meetings will run out of time before getting through each person's material in any meaningful way. Any fewer than four, and you will not have enough input or energy. The idea is that the group is committed to writing and meets once a week. At the meetings, members comment on one another's writing and encourage others. Most groups send new script pages to other members of the group before the meeting so that when they arrive, they have read them, thought about them, and are ready to discuss.

Look for writers' groups within local theater companies. Most theaters have a community of writers working on plays and screenplays, and it is common for these theaters to have weekly meetings you might attend.

Chapter Ten

COMMONLY DEBATED TOPICS

If you join any online screenwriting group, you will find certain topics debated repeatedly, each time with the same ferocious back-and-forth battles over definitions and meaning. Here are some of the commonly discussed topics and the various opinions expressed.

WHERE DO STORY IDEAS COME FROM?

You can find story ideas anywhere. A news item from any source can inspire an idea for a story. A passion to change something in the world can spark an idea. Something that you think would be fun to do can lead to a story idea. Do you have some strong opinion? Turn that opinion into a story by crafting characters that embody that opinion, character(s) the embody a counter opinion, and characters that embody other emotions surround that main opinion and set them at each other's throats. In that conflict, you can illuminate your opinion and possibly comment on the human condition. Ideas are easy to come by. Fleshing that idea out into a compelling story is the work of screenwriting.

WHAT'S THE MOST POPULAR SCREENWRITING SOFTWARE PROGRAM?

Probably, the one most commonly used program is Final Draft. Another favorite is Movie Magic Screenwriter. Screenwriter is a software program created by the company that offers a commonly used production budgeting and scheduling software. Another program is Scriptware.

I have all three programs, and they all are intuitive and offer the writer the ability to seamlessly write treatments, outline, and auto-format a screenplay. And there are many other popular programs that writers prefer for a myriad of reasons, especially for cost.

DO YOU HAVE TO OUTLINE?

The short answer is, no. However, few can craft a quality story without going through a process of treatment and outlining. If you work in television, you will be required to deliver treatments and outlines for approval and notes before scripting. Also, if you get the chance to pitch an unwritten idea, most production companies require treatments and outlines in the development process.

If you feel compelled to skip the treatment and outlining process as you start writing your spec scripts, go for it. I believe that whatever gets you writing and keeps you writing is the most important choice you can make. However, I also believe that you will reach a point in your writing where you find yourself unable to add substantive depth to your writing without going through a treatment and outlining process.

If you truly rebel against this, dive into your writing. However, it will probably take much longer to complete a polished script. Every writer I have met who goes directly to writing script pages without first developing the story through at least an outlining process laments about how many scenes they slaved over that they end up throwing out. Outlining can save you from wasting this creative effort by spotting elements that are unnecessary and eliminating them before you invest a lot of creative juices in writing them.

WHAT IS A THEME, PREMISE, MORAL, OR MESSAGE?

No matter which one of these (theme, premise, moral, or message) is brought up, they all get dragged into the back-and-forth of the thread. Usually, the debate starts when someone new to storytelling asks: What is theme and how do you use it? That's when the fireworks start. To some, theme refers to elements in your story that relate to the human condition, such as honesty, love, compassion, forgiveness. For others, theme is the moral of the story or the story's message, such as Egri's "*Ruthless ambition leads to its own destruction.*" Others argue that theme is not the message at all; they say premise is the story's message.

On and on the thread goes, each person arguing for his or her understanding and, too often, demeaning other points of view. After the first dozen times reading and commenting on a thread on theme, I began to find humor in the ferociously held beliefs. The arguments were the same each time. Now I ignore such threads. It's a waste of time.

The way I approach this part of story development is to understand the distinction between what some call theme topics (honesty, love, compassion, forgiveness, etc.) and a theme that is a message tied to the theme topic. I like to know what my story is about (message-wise) and develop a set of theme topics that I can express or explore in my story that naturally work with my premise or message. (I prefer Egri's thoughts on premise.) Thus, a theme topic of love (or true love) could lead to the central message that: *true love overcomes all obstacles*.

Hopefully, this insight will compel you to study how theme, premise, moral, and message all come into play to help you deepen the impact of your story on an audience.

WHAT DOES "THE DIALOGUE IS ON THE NOSE" MEAN?

"On-the-nose dialogue" is dialogue that has no subtext—such as, when characters say precisely what they think, what they feel or what they see. Here are a couple examples. Case one: A writer describes Paul walking up the street in the action-description. Then in the dialogue, a character says, "Oh, here comes Paul." That's wasted dialogue because the audience knows this visually. Without indicating in the action-description that Paul is walking their way, what if the dialogue between two characters went, "Don't look, now. Here comes Paul," and in the action-description you have the characters turn as if to hide. At least there is some subtext there. Case two: A character says, "I'm mad at you, Paul." That could be an example of boring, on-the-nose dialogue. Instead of saying he or she is mad, have the character take an action that clearly indicates he or she is mad, like slapping or him in the face. Isn't that action far more impactful than the dialogue? *Show before tell*, is the guideline.

Too often, first scripts are riddled with on-the-nose dialogue that feels as if it is written only to fill up pages. The dialogue follows the patter of everyday life conversations but fails to move the story forward. This is fine for your life, but movie dialogue must do so much more.

There are times when on-the-nose dialogue is a good choice, but that is rare and it works best when there is something else going on in the scene that makes the on-the-nose dialogue poignant.

Now, in your first drafts, feel free to write all the junk dialogue that gets your thoughts down on the page. Just clean up and tighten your dialogue in the rewriting passes and give it substance.

WHAT DOES "SHOW, DON'T TELL" MEAN?

As noted above, this is also expressed: *show before tell*. It means that when you have a choice between writing visually (depicting action) and having a character describe something through dialogue, write visually. The adage "a picture is worth a thousand words" is absolutely true in screenwriting. Writing visually is always going to have more impact than talking heads. For example, instead of having a character enter a room and say the place is a mess, describe the scene as a mess and let the character react to the mess and use dialogue to advance the plot. Think visually first.

MAY I USE "WE SEE" IN A SPEC SCRIPT?

The history on this subject is that many scripts written by top screenwriters use the convention of "we see" in describing action, for example, "We see Jack sprint down the hallway," or "We see a hand slip a stack of hundred-dollar bills onto the table." This also applies to "we hear" in the action-description. The complaint by storytelling purists is twofold. First, when a writer uses this convention, it reminds readers that they are reading a script. It's like breaking the fourth wall on stage—this is when an actor acknowledges the audience. The complaint when an unproduced screenwriter uses "we see" or "we hear" is that it comes off as pretentious to some because the writer is using a writing device supposedly reserved for the most successful writers.

Again, as with other elements of non-standard writing rules, if your story is compelling, a reader will overlook the "imperfections," but get rid of them. Challenge yourself, And, as with previous recommendations, feel free to use this convention in your early drafts if it helps you get your story out. Clean it up in the rewrite.

WHAT DOES IT MEAN TO "KILL YOUR DARLINGS"?

This refers to having to cut scenes, dialogue, or other elements in your script that you treasure because the story is better without them. It's common for writers to have to cut some darlings from their scripts to improve them.

WHAT'S A MACGUFFIN (A.K.A. MCGUFFIN, MAGUFFIN)?

A MacGuffin is a plot device, something the writer makes up that the protagonist and the antagonist want desperately and that both sides will take dramatic actions to possess. If you have an idea for a story, but you don't have a clear idea what they could be vying over, make up something and have both sides attach great value to it. That value can be monetary, a relationship, a power the possessor obtains, information, whatever you mind can come up with. Sometimes a writer has a wonderful setting and characters in mind to base an adventure about but does not have a clear idea for a strong central problem for them to conflict over. If this is the case, the writer might invent something. Two examples are, Unobtanium in *Avatar* or the Maltese Falcon statuette in *The Maltese Falcon*.

AS A TELEVISION WRITING SAMPLE, IS IT BETTER TO WRITE AN ORIGINAL TELEVISION PILOT OR TO WRITE A SCRIPT FOR AN EXISTING SHOW?

I've been told that both are acceptable, depending on the show. In some instances, show runners have said they prefer to read an original television pilot. However, most prefer to see that a writer can do solid cover work—that is, that they can write in another's voice. As a television writer, it's your responsibility to match the style of the show's creator. For a television series to be consistent, the episodes must be consistent in tone and visuals. If you do choose to write a sample television script for an existing show, write for a current show that is popular.

To be viable, you will need several writing samples. Make these samples your absolute best work before you submit them. The competition is fierce. Anything less than your best work will leave you on the sidelines.

WHICH IS BETTER, WGA REGISTRATION OR COPYRIGHT?

Copyright registration is promoted on most threads as the most secure way to protect your property. WGA registration is common for the industry. Many writers do both. It seems to me that too many beginning writers waste too much valuable time trying to find a definitive answer to this question. If you are that concerned, do both and get back to writing another script.

CONCLUSION

I realize you can poke holes in many of my thoughts. My purpose was not to write the definitive, in-depth book on industry politics, development or screenwriting. It was to provide some clarity and insights for the beginning screenwriter, a basic lay of the land to dispel some of the mystery—to clear away enough of the fog to see there is a path forward. Hopefully, this book gives you enough insights and confidence to move forward decisively toward your dream of being a working screenwriter.

So much of any business is about who you know and who likes you. This town is no different. As you hone your screenwriting and storytelling skill sets, look to build and nurture industry relationships. If screenwriting is your passion, do as Lew Hunter instructs, "Learn to swim in the deepest end of the pool." Start a daily writing habit. Get involved in the worldwide community and develop relationships. Never stop writing, and never stop networking. Especially, in the beginning. And respect the system.

If I had to pick one word to describe the most valuable career-building commodity in Hollywood, I'd pick: Trust. There is often so much riding on a project that trusting the people who are hired to deliver quality work product and deliver it on time is critical.

Through story, you have the power to change yourself, your lifestyle, and possibly the world. Don't take this profession lightly. On the other hand, don't take it so seriously that you put so much pressure on yourself that it stifles your growth or causes you to take an inordinate amount of time to turn out a polished script.

Now that you have read this book, put it on the shelf and ... Write on!

www.ingramcontent.com/pod-product-compliance
Lightning Source LLC
Chambersburg PA
CBHW032222010526
44113CB00032B/465